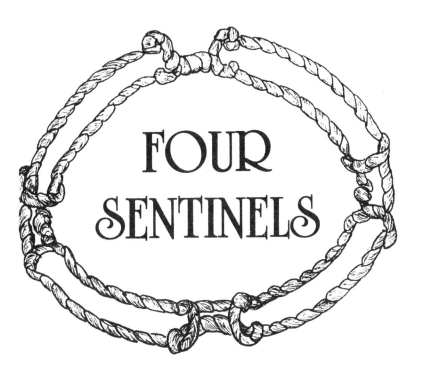

FOUR SENTINELS

The story of San Diego's Lighthouses
with some Lighthouse Recipes

by June Moeser

Library of Congress Catalog Number 91-66002
ISBN 0-938711-10-5

Tecolote Publications
San Diego, California
Printed in the United States of America.

Dedicated to the lighthouse keepers and their families, the United States Coast Guard, the National Park Service, and all who were responsible for maritime safety and the care of lighthouses.

In Memoriam

Muriel Elwood, Freda and Norma Engel, Tom Ham, Jr., Wendell S. Stewart, Joseph W. Worthington, Pat Ziebarth.

Acknowledgements

The following persons are gratefully acknowledged for their assistance in providing me with lighthouse information or recipes, and/or their suggestions for the composition of this book: Thomas A. Balzhiser, A.I.A.; Suzie Ham Bauman, Tom Ham's Lighthouse Restaurant; Carol Bowers, Tecolote Publications; John G. Bunker, Jr., author; D.C. DiGregorio; Madaline Dorsey; Kenneth F. Franke, San Diego Maritime Museum; Pat Fry; Lorenzo Gunn, photographer; Mrs. Tom Ham, Jr.; Sloane Haywood; F. Ross Holland, Jr. National Park Service (ret.); Dan and Christine Lo Russo; Loretta Metzger McCleod; C.F. Moeser; Else O'Neill; Howard Overton, chief ranger, Cabrillo National Monument; Thomas R. Tucker, Sr., superintendent, Cabrillo National Monument (ret.); Bob Wilson, Congressman (ret.); Phillip Winter; Richard B. Yale, Frontier Publishing.

Table of Contents

Foreword. vii
The Guiding Lights. 3
Lighthouses: Ancient History. 9
Old Point Loma Lighthouse. 13
New Point Loma Lighthouse. 19
Ballast Point Lighthouse. 21
Tom Ham's Lighthouse. 27
Lighthouse Food and Recipes. 29

Foreword

The older I get, the more often I encounter interesting knowledge that I should have known about years ago—or perhaps I *was* acquainted with it, but only dimly remember it, if at all, after a hurly-burly pace of eighteen years as Superintendent of Cabrillo National Monument on the tip of Point Loma. June Moeser's fine little book on San Diego's four lighthouses is an example of such knowledge—at once acquainting and re-acquainting me with happenings at the edge of the sea in bygone days.

San Diego's first lighthouse, the old Point Loma lighthouse, is a charming centerpiece for Cabrillo National Monument. It is a living history item and is visited by one and one-half million visitors each year. Visitor comments about the old lighthouse range from "charming" to "rustic environment," and nearly all express the thought that "life was lonely here." June Moeser also captures this quality in her manuscript.

Two of the four lighthouses, the new Point Loma Lighthouse and Tom Ham's Lighthouse, are present-day operating beacons for San Diego's busy maritime activity. A fourth lighthouse, Ballast Point Lighthouse, is no longer in existence.

Lighthouses are about people—people who faithfully kept them and whose solitary lives at the edge of an often tumultuous watery world, exercised a constancy as the welcoming committee for the returning "sailor—home from the sea."

I first knew June Moeser as a charming lady with a passion for painting lighthouse scenes—and what an excellent job she did!

Once June even presented me with a cobblestone from Ballast Point with (you guessed it) a likeness of the old historic Point Loma Lighthouse painted upon it. In 1973, I was privileged along with the National Park Service Associate Director, F. Ross Holland, Jr. (our N.P.S. lighthouse expert), to attend a showing of twenty-four lighthouse paintings by June Moeser at Tom Ham's Lighthouse. We were impressed by June's creative talent in expressing those objects of her love.

Now—she writes about them; and you, like myself, can become re-acquainted with life styles at the edge of the sea.

> Thomas R. Tucker, Sr.
> Superintendent, Retired
> Cabrillo National Monument

Four Sentinels

THE OLD POINT LOMA LIGHTHOUSE 1855
CABRILLO NATIONAL MONUMENT
SAN DIEGO, CALIFORNIA

THE NEW POINT LOMA LIGHTHOUSE 1891
SAN DIEGO, CALIFORNIA

BALLAST POINT 1900
SAN DIEGO, CALIFORNIA

TOM HAM'S LIGHTHOUSE 1971
U.S. COAST GUARD BEACON NUMBER 9
SAN DIEGO, CALIFORNIA

The Guiding Lights

As a student of maritime history, I became more and more intrigued with lighthouses. My curiosity was aroused when I learned of their origin, life cycle, and present status. When I began to draw these historical structures, I could easily see that my paintings were not meant to be architectural renderings. I paint with a free hand and an unacademic eye. In drawing, I sometimes attempt only to suggest the image as it is, or may have been at one time. I think of my paintings as emotional experiences of life, not as fine examples of art.

To paint lighthouses in a natural environment, one must remember that these structures endured more hours of bad weather than good. After all, many of these lights were perched on rugged cliffs, shoals, or monolithic rocks—often apart from land. The words "lonely" and "desolate" are not adequate to describe them. There was always a reason for their isolation, as they were built solely to be "night" and "day" marks for the mariners.

F. Ross Holland, Jr., author of numerous works including *America's Lighthouses,* wrote of one long-time keeper on the Maine Coast who said that the isolation of a lighthouse was hard on a keeper, but it was particularly difficult for the women. The man at least was able to see other people when he went to town to pick up the mail or buy supplies; the wife was confined to her home over much longer periods.

Federal legislation in 1792 stated: "The light in the lighthouse shall be such to distinguish it from others and prevent mistakes." At one time, the count of the world's lighthouses was more than 12,000, each having its own characteristics, rather like a set of fingerprints. John Bunker, noted maritime author, has published numerous articles of lighthouse lore. He wrote, "All lighthouses have a distinguishing characteristic so that the mariner can tell them from other lights in the same general area. Every good navigator carries a copy of the Light list, which tabulates all lighthouses, giving their position and type and sequence of their lights. If a mariner used the Light list in conjunction with reasonably accurate navigation, there is little reason for him to mistake one light for another," ("Beacons of the Sea: A History of Lighthouses," *Oceans,* November 5, 1971).

Looking at them overall, they appear to be similar. Each one is distinctly different, except, perhaps, the twin masonry towers of Chatham Light Station, Massachusetts, built about 1884, and the Navisink twin towers of Mantinicus Rock, Maine, built about 1890.

Early authors did not have cameras to document their writings, and some of these "pharoses" have disappeared through the ages without leaving a trace of an artist's sketch for posterity. Historical writers had to be more descriptive, and their words provide a basis for today's artists who struggle to depict an image from the past. Ancient ship captains tried to have an artist aboard so that the record could be drawn and saved.

This brings to mind the construction of Minot's Ledge, Boston, considered to be "the world's most dangerous lighthouse." It seems incredible that this tower was ever completed. It was built twenty miles southeast of Boston on Cohasset Rocks and was lighted January 1, 1850, and destroyed in a severe storm April 17, 1851. A lightship remained on duty until a new stone tower was lit in 1860. In 1947, this lighthouse was modified to become an unmanned station.

Similar construction and rough seas and storms plagued the California coast light, St. George Reef, near Crescent City. Unbelievable geological hazards and bad weather made the construction of this light a feat almost equal to the building of the Sphinx. Needless to say, the lighthouse keepers had to have the same stamina as their structures to stay on these rock piles.

Minot's Ledge Light Station, Boston, 1845-1848. Collapsed during 1851 storm. New light built and lit November 15, 1860.

(The original painting of this lighthouse is in the private collection of Mr. and Mrs. Phillip Stull.)

St George Reef
Light Station

Samoa-Calif 1891

Each year, more lighthouses are being automated, abandoned, or destroyed. These sentinels have survived bombs, fires, wars, and attacks by Indians. It does not seem right, somehow, to let them die a slow death of erosion or vandalism. This is why I believe that when possible, these old historical lighthouses should be placed in the care of our National Park Service. A successful example is the Old Point Loma Lighthouse, San Diego, designated in 1913 as the Cabrillo National Monument.

When we think of lighthouses as to their importance in our history, we should consider them as part of our maritime American heritage. The late Tom Ham, Jr., San Diego community leader, was very interested in local and maritime history. He recognized the significance of lighthouses when we entered into an agreement to bring lighthouse lore to the public eye. It was 1972, and Tom Ham had just opened his new "official" lighthouse restaurant, Coast Guard No. 9. I agreed to paint twenty-four lighthouses, the majority of them being California lights, for a special showing at his restaurant.

To produce paintings of those lighthouses no longer in existence, I researched documents from the National Archives, history books, and architectural renderings, using whatever sketches, photos, or descriptions I could find. I visited those lighthouses still standing and sketched them on site to be painted later in my studio. One year later, the paintings were ready for their showing at Tom Ham's Lighthouse Restaurant. The paintings were on display a month, and were later viewed at various Navy bases and public buildings. I received hundred of letters and photos from people all over the world who had a special interest in lighthouses. By that time, I had acquired additional knowledge of maritime history and a curiosity and love for those old sentinels that guarded our shore. I never cease to be amazed by the numbers of people who have this fascination for lighthouses. The enrollment of members in organizations such as the U.S. Lighthouse Society attests to this.

My house sits high on a hill overlooking the entrance to the port of San Diego, and I can look out my windows and see the sites of San Diego's four lighthouses. There is a long strip of land that begins near La Playa and bends seaward in a southwesterly direction. This peninsula is known as Point Loma, and for visitors to the Cabrillo National Monument at its tip, the view stretches almost to infinity. In fact, as one scans the horizon, the curve of the earth is very visible. As visitors tour the Old Point Loma Lighthouse, they may note that it was declared out of commission in 1891 because its height of 462 feet above sea level placed it in the way of high fogs which often obscured its light. It was replaced that year by the "new" Point Loma Lighthouse in 1891, less picturesque, but situated at a more functional height on the bluff 300 feet below.

Looking eastward across the bay from the Visitors

Center, tourists' attention is drawn by a push-button voice to Ballast Point below, where (historians have recorded) Juan Rodriquez Cabrillo first set foot on the soil of Alta California in 1542. This narrow strip of land jutting into the entrance of the bay was occupied from 1894-1966 by San Diego's third lighthouse, Ballast Point. An unusual Victorian structure, it was demolished in order that the U.S. Navy could utilize the area. The bell was found later in a scrap metal yard by Alva "Ollie" Oliphant, mechanical art teacher for San Diego City Schools. He purchased it and contacted the family of retired lighthouse keeper Radford Franke to confirm it was the Ballast Point bell. The Oliphants have placed the bell on loan with the San Diego Maritime Museum for public display.

Further across the bay, on the tip of Harbor Island, stands the fourth lighthouse, Tom Ham's Lighthouse Restaurant. More than a seaside cafe, this building houses Beacon No. 9, an operating light commissioned by the U.S. Coast Guard in 1971.

This book was written to commemorate the United States Coast Guard, the keepers and their families, who have shared bits of lore and experiences which I have collected in a continuing fascination with lighthouses.

Lighthouses: Ancient History

For over 2000 years the lighthouse has stood as a symbol of hope and trust. From the first authentic lighthouse, constructed in 311 B.C., men have been guided to safe haven by the welcome flame of a beacon. The Pharos of Alexandria was named after the peninsula on which it was built; "pharos" thus became synonymous with "lighthouse" in the ancient world. Considered to be one of the Seven Wonders of the World, it is still in use today.

It is natural that lighthouses should have originated in the Mediterranean, where commerce flourished when most of the western world still belonged to primitive peoples. In 20 B.C. the Romans built a pharos at Caepio, Spain, and another at Ostia, the port of Rome, seventy-five years later.

By 1600, primitive pharoses were lighting the coasts of Europe. History records the world's best known lighthouse to be the Eddystone Light, built in 1696 on England's shores.

Through the centuries lighthouse keepers have used a variety of materials to keep the lights burning: wood, coal, candles, and a variety of oils—mineral, olive, and whale. Today the "lampie" is giving way to electronics, but man continues to be the "back-up" pilot for each intricate piece of equipment. Under the care of the United States Coast Guard, countless hours have been devoted to manning and maintaining these lonely outposts.

The first lighthouse built in the United States was the Boston Light (1716), but there were no lighthouses on the west coast when California became a state in 1850. Prior to the United States acquiring California at the end of the Mexican War (1848) neither the Spanish or the Mexican governments made any effort to provide beacons or navigational aids to the mariners sailing the Pacific Coast.

In the spring of 1849, the Coast Survey, selected by Congress, recommended sites for the first sixteen lighthouses on the Pacific Coast. Later the Lighthouse Board, created in 1852, and the Treasury Department decided to appropriate monies to construct the lighthouses at the authorized sites. All of the structures had a basic Cape Cod design devised by Ammi B. Young, architect employed by the Treasury Department. The first lighthouses were: Fort Point, Point Bonita, Alcatraz Island, Point Pinos at Monterey, Point Conception, Santa Barbara, the Farrallon Islands off San Francisco, Humboldt Harbor, Crescent City, and Point Loma at San Diego, all in California.

Between 1852 and 1858 others were constructed for Smith Island, Cape Flattery, and Willapa Bay in the territory of Washington and at the mouth of the Umpquo River in Oregon.

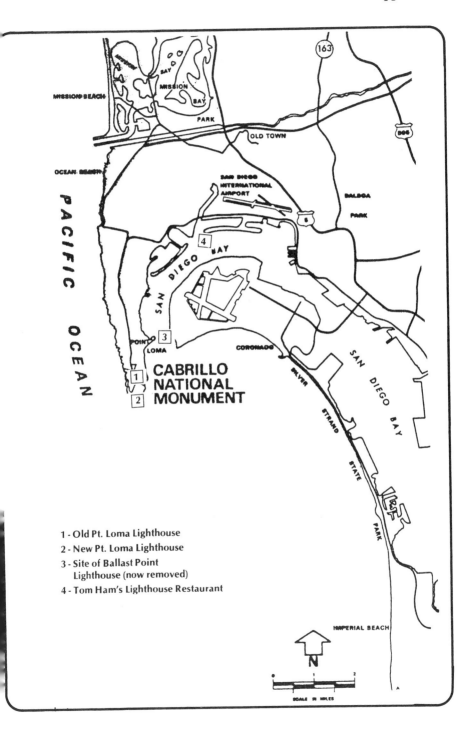

1 - Old Pt. Loma Lighthouse
2 - New Pt. Loma Lighthouse
3 - Site of Ballast Point
    Lighthouse (now removed)
4 - Tom Ham's Lighthouse Restaurant

Old Point Loma Lighthouse, painted by June Moeser, 1973. (Photo by Lorenzo Gunn, 1973.)

Old Point Loma Lighthouse

*"As we made the high point off San Diego, Point
Loma, we were greeted by the cheering presence
of a light-house. As we swept round it in the early
morning, there, before us, lay the little harbor of
San Diego, its low spit of sand, where the water
runs so deep; the opposite flats, where the Alert
grounded in starting for home; the low hills,
without trees, and almost without brush; the quiet
little beach..."*

Richard Henry Dana, Jr.
Two Years Before the Mast

oint Loma was one of the original sites selected
by the U.S. Congress in 1850 to light the Pacific
Coast. In 1852 the government contracted with
Francis. A. Gibbons and Francis X. Kelly of Baltimore,
Maryland, to construct eight lighthouses in California
and Washington. San Diego was one of the locations
selected, and, a little later, Point Loma was deemed the
most desirable site.

On April 7, 1854, the schooner *Vaquero* brought
bricks, cement, lime, and lumber into San Diego
Harbor. Roads had to be built from Ballast Point to
the crest of Point Loma, and, once construction had
begun, water had to be hauled seven miles from La
Playa. Sandstone to mix with the cement was quarried
near Ballast Point, and some of the tiles for the base-
ment floor were obtained from the nearby ruins of the
old Spanish Fort Guijarros. A third-order Fresnel lens,
the highest technology in lights at that time, was

purchased from France. Finally, on November 15, 1855, fifteen minutes before sunset, the Point Loma Lighthouse was lighted for the first time, to begin its 36-year service as the main coastal sentinel to San Diego Harbor. The original construction estimate of $15,000 had ballooned to $30,000, making it the second most costly of the eight lighthouses. In 1854, Oliver S. Witherby, San Diego's first district judge and collector of customs, was appointed superintendent of lighthouses for both Point Loma and Point Conception.

F. Ross Holland, Jr. once described the spectacular view from Point Loma as "One of the three great harbor views in the world." Yet despite its picturesque location and comparatively mild climate, it was not easy to attract keepers to the lighthouse. Pay was low ($1,000 a year in 1855, lowered to $800 a year later), and the transportation of water and supplies up the dirt road was time-consuming. Living quarters were cramped—four small rooms to house the keeper, his assistant, and both their families. To ease the situation, part of the wooden storage out-buildings were converted to living space in the late 1870s. Of the eleven keepers between 1855 and 1891, only four remained longer than one year. Of these, Captain Robert D. Israel performed the longest stint, from 1873 to the lighthouse's abandonment in1891.

What would seem to be a desirable feature of the old lighthouse, its height of 462 feet above sea level, led to its closing in 1891. Although the light was reported to be seen 39 miles out to sea—on a clear night—frequent fogs and low clouds sometimes totally obscured it and rendered it useless. A new site was selected downslope, about 30 feet above sea level.

Within a few years of its abandonment, the lighthouse fell into disrepair; its out-buildings disappeared and the main structure was victimized by vandals. The commanding officer at Fort Rosecrans (which controlled the land on Point Loma except for the lighthouse reservation) recommended converting the building to a radio station. However, the site had become a popular sightseeing spot, and the Order of Panama, a non-profit group, began lobbying for a memorial statue of Cabrillo to be erected. In October 1913, a Presidential Proclamation set aside a half-acre of ground surrounding the lighthouse, designating it as Cabrillo National Monument. The Army made minor repairs to the lighthouse, and it was fully restored by the National Park Service in 1935. The number of visitors increased and were led through the old building by a concessioner.

During World War II, the Army reclaimed the lighthouse and closed it to the public. It was used as a signal station in 1941, and, later in the war, a storage area. It reopened in 1946 with the original concessioner on duty once again. The National Park Service made further improvements and began the process of re-storing the surrounding area to native vegetation.

Thomas R. Tucker, Superintendent of Cabrillo National Monument for eighteen years, oversaw extensive development of the 144 acres. By 1966 construction had been completed on the visitor center view building, auditorium, exhibit room, and admin-istration building. When Tucker retired in 1980, the monument had become an international tourist attraction.

After millions of visitors' treks through the light-house, it once again needed refurbishing. This was accomplished under the administration of Superintendent Doris I. Omundson. Closed to visitors for one year, the restored structure reopened on December 21, 1983. Then, on March 23, 1984, 93 years after his great-grandfather, Captain Robert D. Israel, extinguished the light, David Israel re-lighted the lamp. The light shines inwardly toward the San Diego Harbor from dusk to dawn, 365 days a year, at a candle power level consistent with maritime and air traffic safety requirements.

Today the Old Point Loma Lighthouse, as a distinctive part of the Cabrillo National Monument, receives more visitors than the Statue of Liberty, over 1 million per year. For a small fee or use of a Golden Age Passport, tourists are treated to a panoramic view of the city of San Diego, its harbors, and the outlying islands in the sea. There is an overlook to view the migrating gray whales from December to February, a wonderful hiking area called the Bayside Trail, tidepools, and, of course, the statue of Cabrillo. Historic and scientific information is available in the Visitors Center, which features a bookstore, a museum, and an auditorium for viewing slide shows.

THE OLD POINT LOMA LIGHTHOUSE 1855
CABRILLO NATIONAL MONUMENT
SAN DIEGO, CALIFORNIA

F. Ross Holland, Jr., former National Park Service Superintendent and author of numerous lighthouse books; Author and Artist June D. Moeser; Thomas R. Tucker, Sr., Superintendent Cabrillo National Monument (retired). (Photo by Lorenzo Gunn, 1973.)

New Point Loma Lighthouse, painted by June Moeser, 1973. (Photo by Lorenzo Gunn, 1973.)

New Point Loma Lighthouse

$\mathfrak{L}$acking the Cape Cod quaintness of the Old Point Loma Lighthouse, and the Victorian charm of Ballast Point, the New Point Loma Lighthouse, or the lower light, as it is sometimes called, is simply a tall, metal tube surrounded by a few nondescript buildings. Yet in terms of endurance and service it is the star, having guided ships into San Diego Bay for 100 years.

At 462 feet, the Old Point Loma Lighthouse was the highest in the United States, so high that it was obscured by frequent high fogs while the coast below remained visible. In 1889, the Army transferred land on the lower slope of Point Loma, and also on Ballast Point, to the Lighthouse Board for the construction of two new lighthouses. Construction of the lower light began that same year, and the lighthouse was completed in June 1890. It took a few months to obtain the third-order revolving white lens, which was lit on March 23, 1891, illuminated by a kerosene lamp with three concentric, circular wicks.

Captain Robert D. Israel, who had been the keeper at the Old Point Loma Lighthouse for nearly twenty years, moved to the new lighthouse as its first keeper. However, he remained at that post for less than a year, and then resigned due to some dispute which has been lost in history. On January 9, 1892, George P. Brennan was appointed keeper of the New Point Loma Lighthouse.

In 1911, the fuel for the light was converted from kerosene to kerosene vapor, and then to electricity in

1926. In 1932, command of the light was transferred from the U.S. Lighthouse Service (which would be going out of business in a few years) to the U.S. Coast Guard. Coast Guardsmen who became keepers were allowed to live with their families in a separate house at the lighthouse. Then, in 1973, the lighthouse became totally automated, monitored by computers, and the career of lighthouse keeper became a memory for this lighthouse.

THE NEW POINT LOMA LIGHTHOUSE 1891
SAN DIEGO, CALIFORNIA

Ballast Point Lighthouse

𝕴t nestles like a jewel in the sparkling clean waters at the entrance to San Diego Bay.'' Thus my close friend Norma Engel described the site where her father, Hermann Engel, was keeper from 1914-1931. She took me to visit Ballast Point in 1973, shortly after the opening of my lighthouse art show. We gathered a few old barnacle-covered ballast rocks, and we wondered how many centuries they had lain there. Although the bay waters may not be so pristine as they were then, and the lighthouse since demolished, Norma and I enjoyed the nostalgic experience.

When Radford Franke was offered the position of assistant keeper there in 1929, he asked for advice from his associates about this station of which he had never heard. "Pack your bags—it's the best assignment on the coast!" he was told. Ballast Point was indeed considered a gem of an assignment for keepers.

Ample housing and the warm San Diego climate attracted keepers to Ballast Point. Franke came from Ano Nuevo, an island lighthouse in the sea near San Francisco, regularly lashed by wind and waves, and Engel had come from Point Bonita, situated on the stormy headlands of the Golden Gate. In contrast, Ballast Point, a little spit of land just inside San Diego Harbor, was protected by the cliffs of Point Loma to the west, where the New Point Loma Lighthouse took the brunt of the winds. The housing—roomy Victorian

Ballast Point Lighthouse, painted by June Moeser, 1973. (Photo by Lorenzo Gunn, 1973.)

structures with plenty of space for the keeper, his assistant, and both their families—was far more conducive to family living than the cramped Cape Cod houses that dotted the coast in the first wave of lighthouse construction in the 1850s.

Ballast Point was named for its cobblestones, which early sea captains used as ballast, loading the hulls of their cargo ships with them for the return voyage to the east coast. It is believed to be the site of Juan Rodriguez Cabrillo's first landing on Alta California soil on September 28, 1542. Later, Spanish soldiers built Fort Guijarros nearby and hung a lantern on the point's tip to guide ships into the harbor.

Ballast Point was first lit in 1890, a year before the New Point Loma Lighthouse. David R. Splaine, a former assistant keeper at the Old Point Loma Lighthouse, was the first keeper. Following him in 1898 was James Relue Sweet, an accomplished carpenter who is reported to have built the pilot boat that is still in use on San Diego Bay. Sweet also constructed a house for his dog, matching the Victorian design of the main buildings. His dog was a tenderfoot who suffered so badly from walking over the cobblestones that his master felt compelled to outfit him with leather-padded "slippers." A son was born to the Sweets at Ballast Point Lighthouse, and approximately ten years later Sweet resigned from the U.S. Lighthouse Service to establish his own boatbuilding company.

Hermann Engel's tenure as keeper, 1914-1931, is well chronicled by his daughter in her book. *Three Beams of Light.* Norma Engel was six years old when she arrived at Ballast Point and was given her own small rowboat to paddle around the bay. A favorite occupation of her brothers was to look out from the old Point Loma Lighthouse for incoming ships, and, having spotted one, to race down the harbor, hoping to tag along on the pilot boat. One brother, El, became such a skilled boatman that the pilot captain occasionally let him bring the ships in by himself. El eventually became captain on the Catalina Lines, and then a senior port pilot in Long Beach Harbor. Norma herself interrupted her thirty-five year teaching career with San Diego City Schools to serve in the United States Navy for four years during World War II.

In 1939 Keeper Steve Posaneac and Assistant Keeper Radford Franke enlisted in the Coast Guard, as the U.S. Lighthouse Service was phased out of existence. Franke was promoted to keeper in 1945—the last keeper at Ballast Point.

In 1960 the Congress decided that modern maritime technology had rendered many lighthouses unnecessary and ordered the Coast Guard to dispose of them. Some were left abandoned to erode by time and the elements or vandalism.

Ballast Point was one of the first to be torn down, its remnants sold as junk. The Fresnel lens was saved and is on display at Cabrillo National Monument Visitors Center. Ballast Point has become the site of the U.S. Navy Degauzing Center, which measures the magnetism Navy ships have acquired from their movement through the waters. A high measurement means danger in mine-ridden seas, and such ships are treated with reverse currents to oppose the magnetism before shipping out again.

Artifacts from Ballast Point's history are being collected and restored by the San Diego Maritime Museum, whose executive director, Kenneth F. Franke, is the son of Radford Franke, the last keeper. Kenneth Franke spent his entire childhood at Ballast Point, and, like the Engel children, learned to love the sea. After high school, he attended the California Maritime Academy and the U.S. Coast Guard Officer Training

School, then embarked on a distinguished career in the Coast Guard. In his new position at the Maritime Museum, Franke discovered the old six-foot Ballast Point fog bell at a residence in La Mesa and persuaded its owner, Alva "Ollie" Oliphant, to put it on display at the museum. Franke is on the trail of other lighthouse remnants and information, and by the time the Maritime Museum is moved ot its new Broadway Pier headquarters, he will have created a permanent display to give visitors a glimpse of Ballast Point's history.

Ballast Point Lighthouse—
David R. Splaine, First Keeper 1894

Tom Ham's Lighthouse Restaurant, painted by June Moeser, 1973. (Photo by Lorenzo Gunn, 1973.)

Tom Ham's Lighthouse

$\mathcal{S}$an Diego's fourth and newest lighthouse was the work of the late Tom Ham, Jr. A successful entrepreneur and civic leader, he was dedicated to the preservation of maritime history and San Diego's heritage. His widow, Patricia Ham, is the grand-daughter of Lewis B. Harris, the first Harbormaster of San Diego Bay.

Owner of the Bali Ha'i Restaurant on Shelter Island, Tom Ham's imagination was kindled by a piece of land on the tip of Harbor Island, which he believed would be the perfect setting for a seaport restaurant. Undaunted when the U.S. Coast Guard informed him that he would have to leave an easement on the property for a designated harbor beacon, he decided to enhance the plan by building a lighthouse within his restaurant.

He employed Swank & Associates to construct the building while he gathered maritime art and artifacts, including a dory from Nova Scotia. Tom Ham's Lighthouse Restaurant, with its certified Coast Guard Beacon No. 9, went into service January 1971 and still functions as a lighthouse and a favorite eating and meeting place for San Diegans and tourists.

Tom Ham's special reception, October 1973, initiated the Moeser lighthouse art exhibit. The legions of friends and associates were deeply saddened ten days later when Tom Ham passed away suddenly of a heart attack. The art show exhibited thereafter at various Naval bases and public buildings was in honor of his memory.

The late Tom Ham, Jr. with June Moeser at Tom Ham's Lighthouse Restaurant, 1973. (Photo by Lorenzo Gunn, 1973.)

Lighthouse Food

Ⅎ magine a lighthouse sitting high on a rock pile, miles from shore, with the only mode of transportation a dory or lifeboat. What if weather conditions were violent—lasting for months—how could provisions be maintained or replenished? Lighthouse keepers and wives had to cook with "on hand" ingredients. The trips ashore or to the market might not occur for months. The pantry or larder was usually supplied with products that would not readily spoil. The menu of seafood was interspersed with chicken or turkey from flocks raised on the premises or with dairy products if the keeper had space to keep a cow. Some families were fortunate enough to be situated on land where the ground soil permitted gardening. The usual crops, planted seasonally, consisted of potatoes, tomatoes, carrots, beets, and onions. With these fresh foods and occasional trips to the market, nutritious meals were provided.

Food meant more than nutrition to the keepers and their families. My friend Norma Engel, who lived in three California lighthouses, spoke of the special importance of Saturday nights at Point Bonita Lighthouse, when keepers, assistants, and their families would gather and share a special celebration of doughnuts and coffee. The kitchen was often the main gathering place for the family in late afternoon or early evening and the smell of bubbling beans, a cake or pie baking in the oven, created a sense of well-being and eased the feeling of isolation.

From Norma, her beloved Mother Freda, and many other friends, I have collected some lighthouse recipes. They reflect the simplicity and heartiness of a time gone by. Many times I was privileged to enjoy the home cooking of these magnificent lighthouse ladies in the Engel family and others.

Seafood

Seafood was the most available item on the keeper's menu. At Ballast Point, Norma Engel and her brothers regularly fished in and around San Diego Harbor, and, more often than not, returned home with halibut, bass, sculpin, or some other choice morsel for dinner. They also dug soft-shell clams from the sand and scraped abalone from the rocks. Keeper Hermann Engel trapped lobsters, not only for his family's table, but also to sell as an extra source of income.

Kenneth Franke, son of Keeper Radford Franke, remembers his mother looking at a near-empty larder and saying, "you'd better go out and find a bug." In this case, the "bug" meant a lobster, to be boiled and dipped in butter at the kitchen table. To this day, Franke has trouble thinking of lobster as a gourmet dinner.

Here are some typical lighthouse seafood recipes, featuring a special Seabass recipe from Tom Ham's Lighthouse Restaurant.

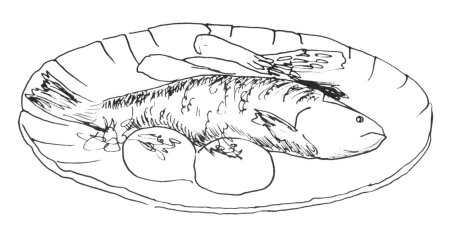

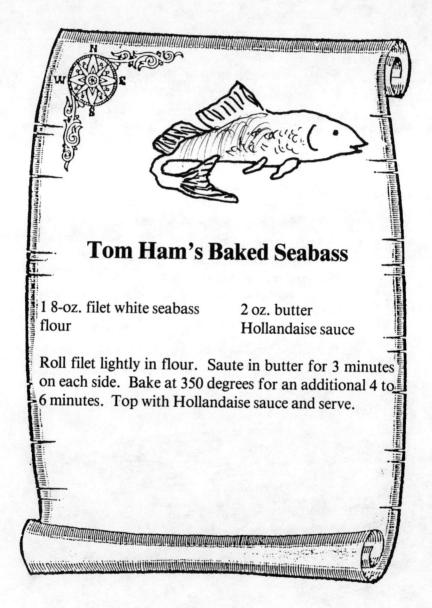

Tom Ham's Baked Seabass

1 8-oz. filet white seabass
flour

2 oz. butter
Hollandaise sauce

Roll filet lightly in flour. Saute in butter for 3 minutes on each side. Bake at 350 degrees for an additional 4 to 6 minutes. Top with Hollandaise sauce and serve.

Baked Codfish

3 cups hot mashed potatoes
1 cup salt cod fish, flaked
⅓ cup melted butter
½ cup cream
1 tsp. scraped onion
½ cup finely chopped green pepper
1 tbsp. minced parsley
salt and pepper

Pre-cook codfish 15 minutes. Combine this with potatoes, butter, cream, and onion. Add minced pepper, parsley, and seasoning to taste. Mix thoroughly. Pour into buttered baking dish. Bake in hot oven (400°) about 20 minutes or until light brown. Should be firm enough to keep loaf form. Garnish with lettuce, olives or pickles cut in fancy shapes. May also be served with white sauce and hard cooked eggs if desired.

Albacore Casserole

½ lb. sliced fresh mushrooms
1 large onion, sliced
chopped fresh parsley
4 to 6 ½-inch slices albacore or bonito*
1 cup dry white wine
½ cup butter
a cup bouillon
juice of 1 lemon
2 tbsp. flour
½ cup cream
1 egg yolk, slightly beaten

Arrange layer of mushrooms in buttered oblong dish or pan, cover with layer of onions, and layer of parsley.

Top with a layer of albacore.

Combine wine, butter, bouillon, and lemon juice. Bring to a boil. Pour over albacore.

Bake in 350° oven for 25 minutes. Drain pan juices, stir in flour.

Mix cream and egg yolk, add gradually. Stir over low heat until thickened and smooth.

Pour over albacore. Serve immediately. Garnish with parsley and paprika if desired. 4-6 servings.

* Canned tuna may be substituted.

Clam Pie

¼ lb. salt pork
1 small onion
1 tbsp. chopped parsley
1/8 tsp. pepper
¼ tsp. celery salt
3 small potatoes

20 small hard clams
2 tbsp. butter
1 cup cream
1 tsp. salt
3 tbsp. flour

Dice the salt pork and let it fry out slowly in a frying pan. Add the finely minced onions and cook until they take on a golden brown color. Strain the clams and to the clam juice add enough water to make 3 cups liquid. Add this liquid to the onion, together with the diced potatoes. Cook about 20 minutes or until the potatoes are tender. Then add the hard clams cut in halves, the fat, celery salt, pepper, and chopped parsley. Blend the flour with 2 tbsp. milk and add to the clam mixture while stirring. Lastly, add 1 cup of cream.

Meanwhile, prepare a rich pastry, using 1 ½ lbs. pastry flour, ⅓ cup shortening, ½ tsp. baking powder, and ½ tsp. salt. Gradually add enough cold water to make a soft dough—about 3 or 4 tbsp. of water will be required. Pour the clam mixture into a greased baking dish and cover with the pastry which has been rolled to fit the baking dish. Bake at 500° for 15 minutes.

Egg and Dairy Dishes

Cows and chickens kept by lighthouse keepers' families often became pets as well as providers of protein, especially when meat sources were scarce (which was frequent). Edward Rowe Snow, in his *Famous Lighthouses of New England,* tells the story of Abbie Burgess, daughter of the Matinicus Rock light keeper. Abbie became a heroine in 1856 when she moved her family to a safe shelter from a building which was destroyed in a fierce storm. She also saved the hens, she reported, "as they were our only companions." The companions returned the favor a year later when Abbie was left to care for her brother while her father was on the mainland for twenty-one days. During his absence, the family was reduced to a daily diet of one cup of corn meal mush and an egg.

The following recipes show the ingenuity of lighthouse cooks in creating interesting meals from egg and dairy products.

Cheese Delight

½ lb. American cheese
5 eggs
1 cup cream
Salt and cayenne

Melt cheese in frying pan, add cream, and salt and cayenne. When thoroughly blended, break eggs onto cheese. Cover for two minutes, then beat briskly for a few moments. Serve immediately. Six servings.

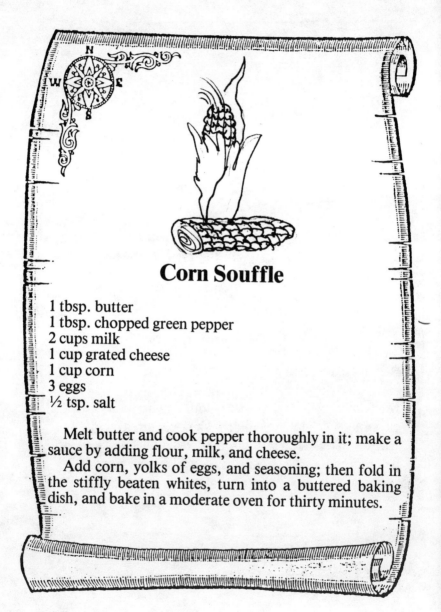

Corn Souffle

1 tbsp. butter
1 tbsp. chopped green pepper
2 cups milk
1 cup grated cheese
1 cup corn
3 eggs
½ tsp. salt

Melt butter and cook pepper thoroughly in it; make a sauce by adding flour, milk, and cheese.

Add corn, yolks of eggs, and seasoning; then fold in the stiffly beaten whites, turn into a buttered baking dish, and bake in a moderate oven for thirty minutes.

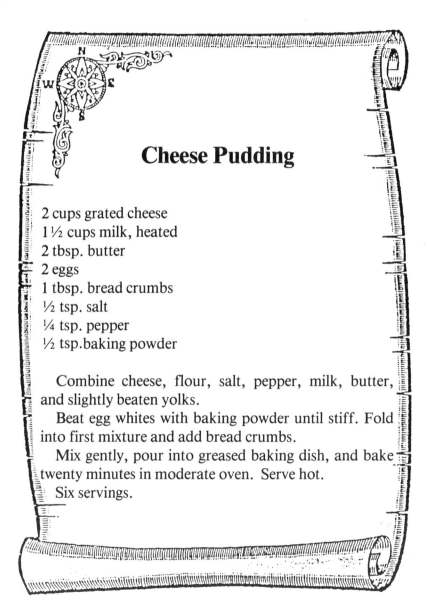

Cheese Pudding

2 cups grated cheese
1 ½ cups milk, heated
2 tbsp. butter
2 eggs
1 tbsp. bread crumbs
½ tsp. salt
¼ tsp. pepper
½ tsp.baking powder

Combine cheese, flour, salt, pepper, milk, butter, and slightly beaten yolks.

Beat egg whites with baking powder until stiff. Fold into first mixture and add bread crumbs.

Mix gently, pour into greased baking dish, and bake twenty minutes in moderate oven. Serve hot.

Six servings.

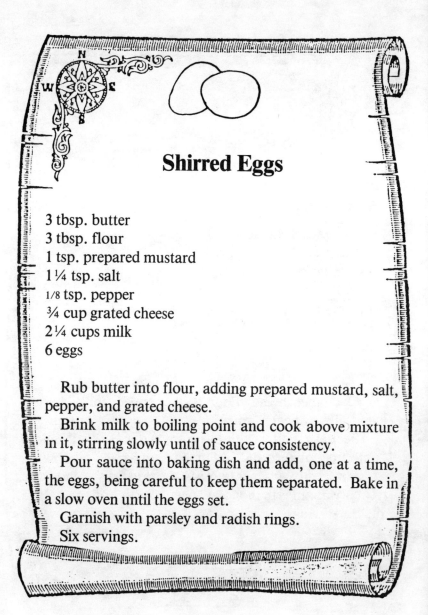

Shirred Eggs

3 tbsp. butter
3 tbsp. flour
1 tsp. prepared mustard
1¼ tsp. salt
1/8 tsp. pepper
¾ cup grated cheese
2¼ cups milk
6 eggs

Rub butter into flour, adding prepared mustard, salt, pepper, and grated cheese.

Brink milk to boiling point and cook above mixture in it, stirring slowly until of sauce consistency.

Pour sauce into baking dish and add, one at a time, the eggs, being careful to keep them separated. Bake in a slow oven until the eggs set.

Garnish with parsley and radish rings.

Six servings.

Cottage Cheese Souffle

2 tbsp. butter
3 tbsp. flour
½ cup milk
½ tsp. salt
Dash cayenne
1 cup cottage cheese
3 eggs
½ tsp. baking powder

Melt butter, add flour, and mix thoroughly. Add milk slowly. Add salt, cayenne, and cheese.

Cook until mixture thickens. Remove from fire and add yolks of eggs beaten light. Cool mixture and mix in baking powder and well-beaten whites.

Pour into greased baking dish and bake in slow oven for thirty minutes. Serve at once.

Four servings.

One-Dish Meals

aked beans were standard fare for lighthouse dinners. Soaked overnight and baked for hours, they were a good source of protein. Innovative casseroles were also created from canned food stocked from infrequent marketing trips. With San Diego's close proximity to Mexico fifteen miles to the south, the Mexican influence made its way into lighthouse recipes, particularly when Mexicans were employed or keepers were married to Mexican descendants. Captain Robert D. Israel, keeper of the Old Point Loma Lighthouse, married Maria Arcadia Alipas, granddaughter of Juan Machado, an early settler and property owner in Old Town, San Diego, where California began. Included in this one-dish section is a recipe for Carne Asada, another gem loaned to us by Tom Ham's Lighthouse Restaurant.

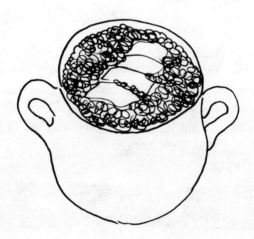

Baked Beans

1 lb. great northern or small white beans
1 qt. boiling water
1½ tsp. salt
1 tsp. dry mustard
½ tsp. freshly ground black pepper
Dash cayenne or Tabasco
½ cup chopped onion
¼ cup molasses or honey
¼ cup brown sugar
¼ cup cider vinegar
¼ lb. salt pork, cubed

Add beans to boiling water; boil 2 minutes; remove from heat and let soak 1 hour. (Or cold soak in cold water overnight, if desired.) Drain beans.

Combine dry ingredients and mix well with beans. Stir in Tabasco, onion, molasses, brown sugar, and vinegar. Pour half of the 6-cup mixture into a 1½-to 2-quart baking dish.

Add half the pork in a layer, then the rest of the beans. Top with a final layer of pork. Pour in boiling water to reach the top of the beans. Cover and bake at 300° for 6 hours.

Add a little boiling water if needed during baking to keep beans from drying out.

Tom Ham's Carne Asada

3 pieces thinly sliced filet   cottonseed oil
  mignon (approx. 8 oz.)   1 cup red wine
cuminos   paprika
garlic   Mexican oregano

Marinate filets in mixture of cottonseed oil, spices, and red wine for at least one hour. In a hot skillet or grill, cook filets for 60 to 90 seconds on each side. Serve with spiced vegetables, Spanish rice, and guacamole.

Corn Scallop Casserole

2 ½ cups corn
1 cup milk
1 well beaten egg
¾ tsp. salt
1/8 tsp. pepper
1 ½ cups cracker crumbs
¼ cup minced onion
3 tbsp. chopped pimiento
2 tbsp. butter

Cook corn until tender, drain. Heat cooked corn with milk, gradually add egg and all seasonings. Add 1 cup cracker crumbs. Mix well.

Pour in greased 8 ½ x 1 ¾ round cake pan or casserole. Melt butter, pour over ½ cup crumbs, and sprinkle over top of casserole.

Bake at 350° for 40 minutes. Garnish with pimiento. Serves 6.

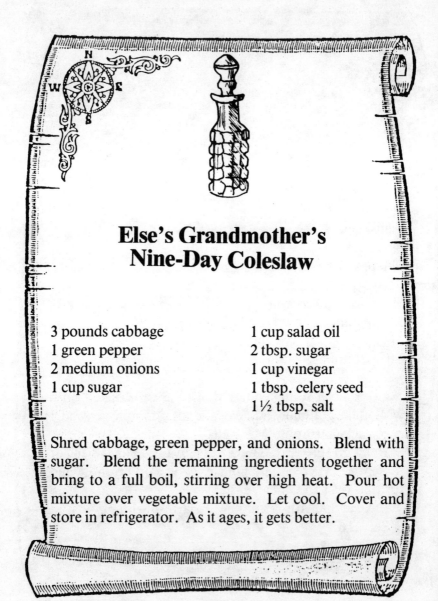

Else's Grandmother's Nine-Day Coleslaw

3 pounds cabbage
1 green pepper
2 medium onions
1 cup sugar

1 cup salad oil
2 tbsp. sugar
1 cup vinegar
1 tbsp. celery seed
1½ tbsp. salt

Shred cabbage, green pepper, and onions. Blend with sugar. Blend the remaining ingredients together and bring to a full boil, stirring over high heat. Pour hot mixture over vegetable mixture. Let cool. Cover and store in refrigerator. As it ages, it gets better.

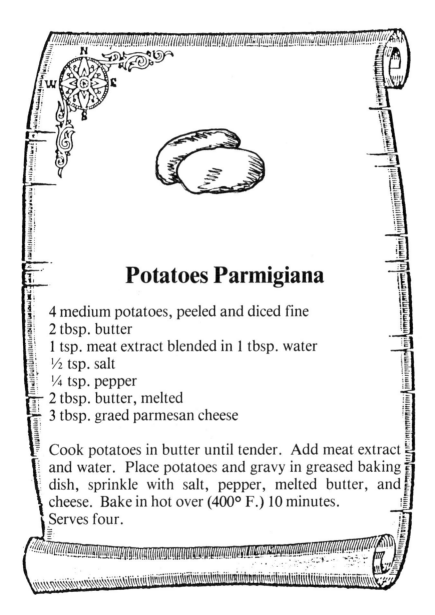

Potatoes Parmigiana

4 medium potatoes, peeled and diced fine
2 tbsp. butter
1 tsp. meat extract blended in 1 tbsp. water
½ tsp. salt
¼ tsp. pepper
2 tbsp. butter, melted
3 tbsp. graed parmesan cheese

Cook potatoes in butter until tender. Add meat extract
and water. Place potatoes and gravy in greased baking
dish, sprinkle with salt, pepper, melted butter, and
cheese. Bake in hot over (400° F.) 10 minutes.
Serves four.

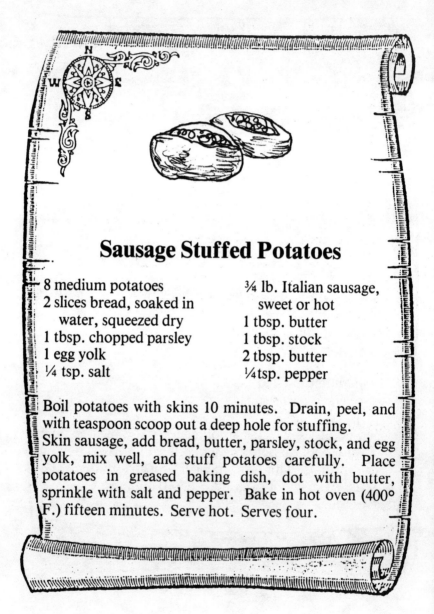

Sausage Stuffed Potatoes

8 medium potatoes
2 slices bread, soaked in
   water, squeezed dry
1 tbsp. chopped parsley
1 egg yolk
¼ tsp. salt

¾ lb. Italian sausage,
   sweet or hot
1 tbsp. butter
1 tbsp. stock
2 tbsp. butter
¼ tsp. pepper

Boil potatoes with skins 10 minutes. Drain, peel, and with teaspoon scoop out a deep hole for stuffing.
Skin sausage, add bread, butter, parsley, stock, and egg yolk, mix well, and stuff potatoes carefully. Place potatoes in greased baking dish, dot with butter, sprinkle with salt and pepper. Bake in hot oven (400° F.) fifteen minutes. Serve hot. Serves four.

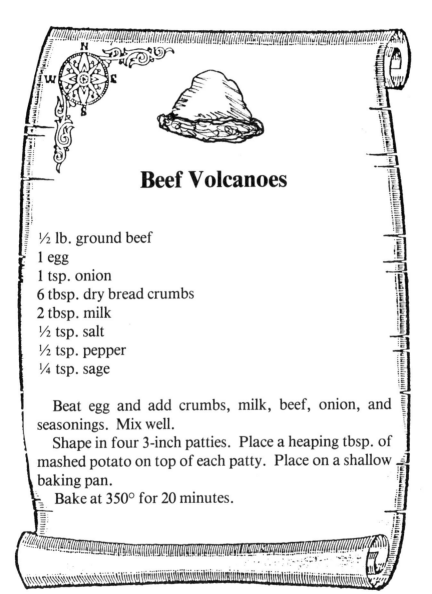

Beef Volcanoes

½ lb. ground beef
1 egg
1 tsp. onion
6 tbsp. dry bread crumbs
2 tbsp. milk
½ tsp. salt
½ tsp. pepper
¼ tsp. sage

Beat egg and add crumbs, milk, beef, onion, and seasonings. Mix well.

Shape in four 3-inch patties. Place a heaping tbsp. of mashed potato on top of each patty. Place on a shallow baking pan.

Bake at 350° for 20 minutes.

Baked Lima Beans

1 lb. dry lima beans
2 cups fresh or canned tomatoes
1 tsp. salt
½ tsp. paprika
2 slices bacon or salt pork (diced)

Soak the beans overnight in water to cover, then cook in salted boiling water until just tender, but not broken.

Drain the beans, and add tomatoes and seasonings and turn into casserole or bean pot, putting the bacon or pork on top.

Cover and bake in 350° oven one hour.

Marmalade Ham Loaf

1½ lbs. fresh pork, ground
1½ lbs. ham, ground
¾ loaf dry bread, cubed
2 cups milk
½ cup chopped onion
½ tsp. thyme
½ tsp. sage
¼ tsp. salt
1 tsp. dry mustard
¼ tsp. cinnamon
¼ tsp. cloves
1 cup orange marmalade
2 tbsp. vinegar

Toss dry bread cubes with thyme, sage, and salt. Soak in milk for five minutes.

Lightly brown meats and onion in skillet. Drain and add to milk mixture. Lightly pack in 9 x 9 x 2 baking dish.

Bake in moderate oven (350°) for 1¼ hours. Spoon off drippings.

Mix together marmalade, vinegar, mustard, cinnamon and cloves. Spread over loaf, return to oven, and bake 10 minutes longer. Let stand a few minutes before cutting into squares. Top with orange slices.
Serves 9-12.

Baked Goods

With wood-burning stoves whose temperatures were tricky to maintain, keepers' wives turned out the daily bread and sumptuous desserts for special occasions. The following samples include "the best apple pie in the world," developed by my friend and fellow lighthouse *aficionado* Thomas A. Balzhiser, whose favorite lighthouse is Heceta Head Lighthouse in Oregon.

Heceta Lighthouse, Oregon coast

Tom's Apple Pie

Pastry:

Day before, place in refrigerator to chill:
One three-quart mixing bowl containing:
    3 cups all-purpose flour
    1 tsp. salt mixed into flour
One measuring cup containing:
    1 cup butter-flavored vegetable shortening
Baking day, to chilled flour mixture cut in shortening until oat-like in appearance.

In another bowl, quickly combine:
    1 chilled, beaten egg
    6 tbsp. ice cube-chilled milk
    1 tbsp. lemon juice or white vinegar
Stir into flour mixture quickly, gather into ball, kneading lightly so dough just sticks together. Divide into two parts, flatten each half to make thin disk. Wrap each in plastic, refrigerate for 30 minutes before rolling out. Line nine-inch pie pan, handling as little as possible.

Filling:

Combine in large bowl:
    1 cup brown sugar, packed
    ⅓ cup granulated sugar
    2 tbsp. flour
    ⅔ tsp. cinnamon
Then, cut in
    1 tbsp. butter or margarine until crumbs form. Add 6 cups peeled and sliced tart apples (about 2 pounds). Pour mixture into pie shell and sprinkle with 4 tbsp. apple cider. Add top crust, patterned or latticed, brush top with milk, and sprinkle with sugar.

Bake in preheated 400-degree oven for 10 minutes; reduce heat to 375 degrees for 35 minutes more baking time. Cool to room temperature and serve with scoop of French vanilla ice cream.

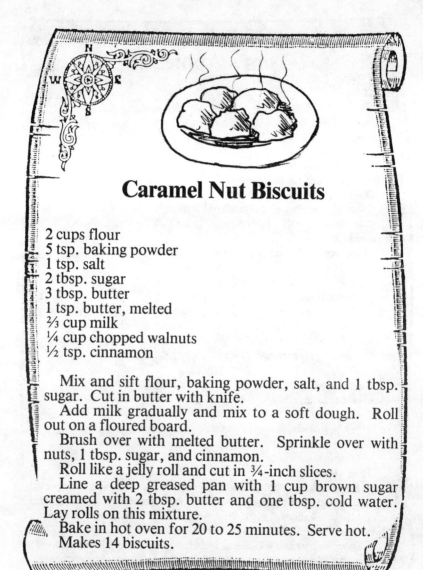

Caramel Nut Biscuits

2 cups flour
5 tsp. baking powder
1 tsp. salt
2 tbsp. sugar
3 tbsp. butter
1 tsp. butter, melted
⅔ cup milk
¼ cup chopped walnuts
½ tsp. cinnamon

Mix and sift flour, baking powder, salt, and 1 tbsp. sugar. Cut in butter with knife.

Add milk gradually and mix to a soft dough. Roll out on a floured board.

Brush over with melted butter. Sprinkle over with nuts, 1 tbsp. sugar, and cinnamon.

Roll like a jelly roll and cut in ¾-inch slices.

Line a deep greased pan with 1 cup brown sugar creamed with 2 tbsp. butter and one tbsp. cold water. Lay rolls on this mixture.

Bake in hot oven for 20 to 25 minutes. Serve hot. Makes 14 biscuits.

Scotch Scones

2 cups flour
3 tsp. baking powder
1 tsp. salt
2 tbsp. sugar
3 tbsp. butter
¾ cup butter
¾ cup milk
2 eggs

Sift together flour, baking powder, salt, and sugar. Rub in butter with finger tips. Beat eggs very light, add to milk and add slowly to first mixture. Roll to half-inch thickness, cut into squares and fold over, make into triangle. Brush with milk and bake on greased pan about 20 minutes in hot oven. Currants or raisins may be added for variation.

Refrigerator Cookies

1 cup butter, softened
1 cup sugar
2 eggs
1½ tsp. vanilla

3 cups sifted, all
   purpose flour
1 tsp. salt
½ cup chopped nuts

Mix butter, sugar, eggs, and vanilla. Stir in flour and nuts. Divide dough into 3 parts, each about 7 inches long. Wrap and chill at least 4 hours.
Heat oven to 400° Cut rolls into 1/8-inch slices. Place on ungreased pan. Bake 8 to 10 minutes or until light brown. Immediately remove from baking sheet. Makes about 7 dozen cookies.

Refrigerator Spice Cookies

½ cup butter
1 cup dark brown sugar
  (packed)
1 egg
1 tsp. vanilla extract
2½ cups all purpose
  flour

½ tsp. soda
¼ tsp. salt
1 tsp. cinnamon
½ tsp. nutmeg
1 cup nuts

Cream butter and sugar until light and fluffy. Beat in egg and vanilla. Sift flour, measure and sift again with soda, salt, cinnamon, and nutmeg. Stir into butter-sugar mixture. Add nuts, mix well. Shape into roll; wrap in waxed paper and chill. Cut into thin slices and bake on lightly greased baking sheet in 350° oven 8-10 minutes.
Makes 6 to 7 dozen cookies.

Buttermilk Pie

Dough for a one-crust
  9-inch pie
1 cup sugar
3 tbsp. flour
3 eggs, beaten
1 tbsp. grated lemon
  zest

4 tbsp. butter, melted
  and cooled
1 cup buttermilk
½ tsp. vanilla extract
2 tbsp. lemon juice
½ tsp. grated nutmeg

Preheat oven to 425 degrees.
Line pie pan with dough. Prick with fork and press a piece of aluminum foil snugly into the pan, covering the dough. Bake 6 minutes. Remove foil. Bake 4 minutes more, until edges of crust begin to turn pale brown. Remove from oven and cool.
Mix together sugar and flour. Beat in eggs, then melted butter, buttermilk, vanilla extract, lemon juice, and zest.
Pour filling into cooled shell and bake (at 425 degrees) 10 minutes. Sprinkle top with nutmeg. Lower temperature to 350 degrees and bake 30 minutes more, or until knife inserted in center comes out clean.
Remove from oven and cool. (Center will deflate as pie cools.) Serve lukewarm, but refrigerate leftover pie.

Ice Box Rolls

¾ cup lard, melted.
1 cup hot mashed
   potatoes.
3 tbsp. sugar.
2 tsp. salt.

3 eggs, beaten
1 cup milk, scalded.
½ cup lukewarm water with yeast
   cake dissolved in it.
Flour, as needed.

Mix melted lard, beaten eggs, hot milk, potatoes, sugar, and salt. Let stand until cool. Then add water with yeast cake in it. Stir flour into this mixture until it is too stiff to stir, then turn out on board and knead. Put in greased pan with lid on and let stand in frigidaire overnight. Then make out rolls as needed. Rolls should be made out 3 to 4 hours before baking.

Apple Delight

6 to 8 apples
½ cup sugar
2 tbsp. water
1 cup uncooked oats
½ cup brown sugar

½ tsp. cinnamon
2 tbsp. chopped nuts
1 tsp. greated lemon rind
4 tbsp. melted butter or
    margarine

Pare, core, and slice apples into a shallow baking dish. Add sugar and water (or use lemon juice in place of water if apples are not very tart). Place in a moderate oven (350? F.) to heat while you combine remaining ingredients, mixing thoroughly. Spread over apples and bake about 45 minutes, or until apples are tender and crust browned. Serve warm or cold, with top milk. Serves six.

A typical lighthouse keeper's uniform of early days.

Bibliography

John Bunker, "Beacons of the Sea: a History of Lighthouses," *Oceans Magazine,* October, 1971.

Norma Engel, *Three Beams of Light,* Tecolote Publications, 1986.

John J. Floherty, *Sentries of the Sea,* J.P. Lippincott Co., 1942.

Jim Gibbs, *West Coast Lighthouses*, Superior Publishing Co., 1974.

F. Ross Holland, Jr., *America's Lighthouses,* Stephen Green Press, 1972.

Fred Majdalany, *The Eddystone Light,* Houghton Mifflin, 1960.

George R. Putnam, *Lighthouses and Lightships of the United States,* Houghton, 1917.

Edward R. Snow, *Famous Lighthouses of America,* Dodd, 1953, and *Famous New England Lighthouses,* Yankee Publishing Co., 1945.